# So You Think You Can Be President?

**What Donald Trump's
Campaign Can
Teach You about Winning
in the Era of Reality TV**

**by Marion TD Lewis**

To Mr Trump, his friends and his foes

## INTRODUCTION

I wrote this book in 2015 during the fall when the presidential primaries were in full swing and Mr Trump, though slipping in the polls, was still the dominant candidate among Republicans and even polling well against Hillary Clinton in the national polls (though she was still ahead).

Why did I write this book? Well, I have always been fascinated by Mr Trump and so when he decided to run for president, I followed his every move. The tone of this book is meant to be quasi funny, quasi serious because indeed that is how I viewed Mr Trump. I found him to be a dual and mercurial personality whose politics could be scary and outrageous though also funny and inspirational. (Truth be told, sometimes the inspiration was more along the lines of what NOT to do or say.) As of this writing, the elections are still a full year away so there is no way for me to predict the outcome. So much could happen between now and next November. In the meantime, while we all wait with baited breath to see how this turns out, this book can serve as a manual for people who are trying to achieve success in their lives. They may not be running for president but maybe they need to outperform a colleague for a promotion; or they are trying to win a part in an off Broadway play; or there is anything at all they want to win at.

The thing with Mr Trump and the way he ran his campaign is that it is clear we are living in a new era where traditional rules have been turned on their heads. It is no longer a virtue to be polite and politically correct (if you can get away with doing the opposite and getting ahead). Remember the saying "nice guys finish last?" This seems to be truer today than ever before and Mr Trump's strategies and techniques clearly proved that. Even if he does not make it to the White House, he clearly has proven that in the digital/technological/social media/reality TV era, the rules of the game for "winning" in life have probably been changed forever.

# Table of Contents

8.  Master the Sound Bite

9.  Shock 'em

10. Refuse to Be Politically Correct

11. Look Distinctive

12. Befriend Your Enemies

13. Have a Hot Spouse or an Even Hotter

    Daughter

14. Use Third Grade Vocabulary

15. Wing It

16. Never Use Teleprompters

17. Fire Your Campaign Staff if They Get

    on Your Nerves

18. Hire Scary Lawyers and PR People

19. Gain a Psychological Edge by Hook or Crook

20. Use You Private Residence (which must be posh) as your campaign Headquarters

21. Threaten to Run Independent if the Party You Are Running Under Fails to Treat You Fairly

22. Give out your Opponent's Private Cell Phone Number on National TV (and other pranks)

23. Sleep as Little as Possible

24. Master the Art of the Pivot

25. Donate to Politicians From Both
    Parties Then Publically Shame the
    Recipients of your Cash

26. Make Big Promises Even If You Can't
    Keep Them

27. Have a Full Head of Iconic Hair

28. Have a Catchy Campaign Slogan

29. Admit to An Erratic Voting Record

30. Lower Expectations While
    Simultaneously Raising Expectations

31.Do Not Fundraise

32.Make It Up As You Go Along

33.Hire a young, hungry Campaign

Manager

34.Be Frugal

35.Intimidate by Suing People Left and

Right

36.Pay Actors if Necessary

37.Blame Other Countries for Your

Country's Economic Woes

38.Be up Front About Not Liking to

Shake Hands

39. Promise to Be a Bomb Thrower

40. Promise to Create Jobs For the People

   You Insult

41. Constantly Tell the Media They Suck

42. Whine A Lot

43. Hire a Sexy Assistant

44. Load Up on Energy

45. Be a Bully

46. Master the Art of the Multiple

   Personality

47. Be Unpredictable

48. Promise to Lower Taxes for Everyone

49. Don't Hesitate to Dig Up and Release

    All the Dirt You Can Find On Your

    Enemies

50. Have an Exit Strategy Long Before

    You Need It

## 1. Have a Great Last Name
## Or, Make One Up

A catchy name can determine your fate – especially your presidential fate. The name TRUMP, for example, has a lot of "nominative determinism" and it was one of Mr Trump's main assets in the 2016 presidential campaign. Everyone has to agree that the name TRUMP is a great, fortuitous name. But check this out: T.R.U.M.P. was not the original spelling used by the Trump ancestors, interestingly enough.

You see, Mr Trump is a descendant of Scottish immigrants on his mother's side and German immigrants on his father's side. His paternal great grandfather's name was Drumpf not Trump, but the name was changed to Trump sometime during the life of Mr Trump's great grandpa Johannes Christiane Drumpf – a proud German. It was a smart decision on Mr Drumpf's part and was incredibly fortuitous for Mr Trump as we know the reality TV mogul today. The word Trump literally means "to outrank or defeat someone or something, often in a highly public way." What better name could there possibly be for someone who is running for president? The lesson is that if your family name is not sufficiently anglicized and catchy, change it to something that sounds like a winner and do it at least one or two generations before you run, if possible.

## 2.  Have Your Own Private Jet

Mr Trump has a fleet of air transportation that includes helicopters and aircrafts that include a 747 corporate jet. All of his wheels/wings have his family name TRUMP emblazoned on the sides. When he landed at the Iowa State Fair in summer 2015, he emerged from his eponymous helicopter (which he then used to fly little Iowan children handpicked by the campaign for a helicopter ride over the grounds while they called him "batman") like a rock star. Ditto for when he landed in Cleveland for the first debate. He emerged from his Boeing 747 behind his wife, a former Slovenian model named Melania. They, along with his comely brood of children, descended the steps of the aircraft like American royalty to greet the press who were waiting for them below. It was a heck of an entrance. None of the other candidates could compete with the movie star entrance and the appeal of Mr

Trump. Needless to say, the whole event from start to finish was the Trump Show. There is no telling how many votes he won just by that entrance alone but it should be noted that after the first debate in Cleveland and in spite of a post-debate controversial Twitter feud with one of the debate moderators, Megyn Kelly, Mr Trump poll numbers went up, up, up.

### 3. Brag Shamelessly

When Mr Trump announced his run for the presidency of the United States, he started with a multi-billion dollar brag: "I am rich." Indeed, he had a sheet of paper which he said had been created by his accountants and which he said showed his financial net-worth. However, when he officially released his financials a few weeks later, it said he was worth a whopping ten billion dollars, even more than he had announced on the piece of paper when he launched his bid. So his net-worth went up in a very short time (according to him) and he never let anybody forget it. His net-worth is hardly the only thing Mr Trump bragged about.

He constantly reminded everyone of his alma mater The Wharton School of Finance in Pennsylvania. It may not be Harvard but Mr Trump never let anyone forget that Wharton is the "hardest school to get into." He also bragged about his best-selling book, "the Art of the Deal" and other things, like his ability to generate huge ratings and the fact that he gave a lot of politicians (including some of his challengers) a lot of money over the years. He also bragged shamelessly about his beautiful daughter Ivanka (though interestingly never about his youngest daughter named Tiffany); and of course he bragged about his beautiful supermodel wife Melania. He bragged a lot about having the best golf courses; buildings and hotels around the world and he even bragged that he would get along with Russian president Vladimir Putin. Mr Trump showed no shame about his bragging tendencies. It is what gave him his competitive edge.

He only ever spoke in superlatives. Everything he owns, in his opinion, is the best. He has admitted that he loves saying that he is the best and what he owns is the best. People pretended to be put off, but they must have been secretly impressed because they kept him very high in the polls for a very long time. So the lesson is, even at the risk of being called a braggart you have got to toot your own horn.

## 4. Know How to Hand the Media Their Posterior in a Tweet

Mr Trump had well over 3 million followers on Twitter when this book was published and he regularly engaged with them, tweeting and retweeting on a daily basis. So they became like good friends so that when he was attacked in the media, he was able to go on his Twitter and get support. This support was powerful because these people have purchasing power and could threaten to boycott businesses or networks that spoke badly about Mr Trump. Sometimes they even allegedly sent death threats, such as for example in the case of Megyn Kelly, the Fox News debate moderator.

Nobody, not even the Media, messed with Mr Trump without accepting the consequences which usually was a kick in the posterior and/or a slap in the face (metaphorically speaking). People seemed to be very afraid of Mr Trump and this was probably because they knew that without a huge amount of provocation, he would hand them their asses and knock them on their bellies like little puppy dogs for everyone to see. Look at how Fox News bowed down to him after the Megan Kelly brouhaha.

The president of the network Roger Ailes literally called Mr Trump and allegedly promised Mr Trump that Fox News would "treat him fairly going forward." Why did this move become necessary? Because Ms Kelly had "behaved badly." She had dug up past derogatory comments Mr Trump had made to women and confronted him with those words in the Cleveland debate, audaciously asking Mr Trump if he was "part of the war on women." Though Mr Trump had indeed used the epithets Kelly dug up to various women, he did not appreciate being put on the spot in front of 24 million people who were watching the debate and so after the debate, he launched an aggressive attack on Ms Kelly on social media, primarily on his Twitter account. The next thing that happened was that Fox News and their bosses got on their knees and begged for forgiveness and Trump continued to attack Megyn and Fox every chance he got. The lesson? Give 'em hell and only then will they respect you.

## 5. Be an Insult Artist

Who didn't experience the brunt of a Trump-dusted insult? Who was not criticized and called "stupid" "idiot" and "lightweight" "Incompetent"? What about "look at that face" the zinger he lanced at Carly Fiorina? Of Rand Paul he famously deadpanned, "I never attacked his looks but believe me there is plenty of subject matter there!" Yes, he got a lot of criticism for this tendency he has and many people publicly frowned at his bad manners.

But secretly they must have been amused or entertained because none of these outburst had any negative impact on Mr Trump's poll numbers. It is kind of like he was saying all the things people wished they could say but did not have the courage to say because, well, it is considered bad manners. But Mr Trump did not care what he said and who he said it to.

No one was immune to his attacks and insults. Not even war heroes like John McCain. By challenging John McCain's record as a war hero, and staying at the top of the polls afterwards, Mr Trump demonstrated that being unafraid to challenge the status quo or to question long held opinions or more directly to challenge the record of a decorated American veteran can be done (even if what you say is insulting) and can even be a winning strategy. The way it seems to work is that the insulter has to remain steadfast, has to double and triple down after demands for apologies ("I will apologize when I say or do something wrong," Mr Trump famously said) and say what your audience wants to hear. For example, one time Mr Trump insulted Marco Rubio calling him "a clown." The audience did not want to hear that insult levelled at Mr Rubio and they booed Mr Trump.

By contrast he has said much worse about others and received standing ovations. So one must consider the audience and be sure it is what the audience wants to hear before levelling the insult. The key to this strategy is timing. Insults have to be well timed. But you also have to know who to insult and when to insult them.

## 6. **Never Apologize**

How many times was Mr Trump called upon to apologize for something awful that he had said, some slur he had levelled or some insult he had hurled? Countless times. How many times did he actually follow through with an apology? Exactly. His refusal to apologize even when it seemed that the most hard core person would have buckled under pressure was another reason that he continued to gain new supporters.

People viewed this as "toughness." They called him a "fighter." Apologies are for sissies he seemed to say, continuing with the same objectionable rhetoric or sometimes even going so far to say that it was the person he was being asked to apologize to who owed *him* an apology. It was incredibly creative the way he used words as a sort of currency and weapon simultaneously to create ideas – however objectionable some of it might have been. If there were casualties along the way, such that feelings were hurt or reputations called into question then he seemed to say "deal with it." Eventually, people stopped demanding that he apologize.

### 7. Throw 'em under the Bus

When necessary, throw them under the bus à la Mr Trump. He never hesitated to publicly shame his opponents or bring up their faults and weaknesses or shift blame to them whenever he was blamed for a misdeed or when he felt ambushed. One classic example is when the furor over "the war" on women erupted and the media tried to paint Mr Trump as a woman hater after he made certain comments about Fox News moderator Megyn Kelly. He said something to the effect of "she had blood coming out of her eyes...blood coming out of her wherever..." His opponents jumped on the bandwagon to criticize and condemn him but he just turned right around and blamed Jeb Bush for hating women. He said that it was Jeb Bush was the one who hated women since Jeb had said he would not spend more than a certain amount on women's health.

Then Trump promised to take care of women and said that he "cherishes" women and that he would be "phenomenal to women." He repeated this over and over. To drive the point home, Trump put out a video of Bush's own mother Barbara

Bush in which she is seen saying that she didn't think the country needed another Bush for president. It was very hard for Jeb after that. He just began to tank in the polls like nobody's business.

## 8. Master the sound bite

To stay at the top of the polls you have to be a media darling and to do that you have to be good with the one-liners. Mr Trump was very good at the sound bite. Usually, it was an insult packaged in a tweet-sized diss.

He excelled at this; it was his "wheel horse." He reiterated the same lines enough times that eventually, the repetition makes it sound like truth and people begin to associate the sound bite with reality. One of his best one liners was "Jeb is low energy."

Another time he said about Carly Fiorina "look at that face." Another time he said of Rand Paul "I never criticized his looks even though there is plenty of subject matter there." Trump was also very good with his timing. This is critically important for budding presidential wannabes who want to use soundbites to their advantage. The key thing to remember is that it is not what you say or even how you say it, but *when* you say what you say that could make the difference with how the message is received and digested by the public.

And it is not just being able to put others down it is knowing exactly when and how to do it so that no matter what happens after, you will be eventually forgiven by the press and the public who usually could be counted on to demonize the victim once Mr Trump was through with his latest victim.

## 9. Shock 'em

Mr Trump could be very shocking. He often left people slack jawed with…shock. They would sit there with their mouths agape completely unable to believe that that not only had he said or done something, but that he had gotten away with it. He shocked and he got away with it and he shocked some more and then he was too compelling to ignore. People wanted to hear what he would say next. People viewed his getting away with it as evidence that he was "tough" and a "fighter."

For example, when he launched and pursued the birther movement against Barack Obama and then refused to correct the record during the campaign, this was shocking; when he called Mexican immigrants rapists it was shocking; when he disclosed the private cell phone number of Lindsey Graham it was shocking; when he made the blood comments about Megyn Kelly it was shocking. Mr Trump left an indelible visual in people's minds. He had no filter and many people found this very refreshing and compelling. These folks really liked this aspect of the candidate. They liked being shocked by Mr Trump. It got their adrenaline pumping and they became bolder and more shocking in their own public outburst as well.

## 10. **Refuse to be Politically Correct**

Mr Trump was unapologetically politically incorrect. He has said that he has no time for political correctness and that America also could not indulge in the luxury of political correctness either. In fact, you could say that he made it cool to be rude. It is not just being able to put others down it is knowing exactly when and how to do it so that no matter what happens after, you will be eventually forgiven by the press and the public who usually could be counted on to demonize the victim once Mr Trump was through with the unlucky lad or lass.

His entire brand image rested on this image of brashness and bluntness and "telling it like it was." Many people equated political correctness with glib politicians who are all talk and no action. Mr Trump was seen as an action man with little time for niceties. The proof of the success of this approach was in his net-worth statement. Americans knew that his style had worked for him and they admired him rather than disdained him for this personality trait. Before you knew it, more people were talking about political correctness as if it were a dreaded disease. And the more politically incorrect Mr Trump got, the higher he climbed in the poll.

## 11. Look Distinctive

In his youth, Mr Trump was a very handsome, very virile German/Scottish American playboy. As he aged, his looks arguably receded a little bit. But this probably helped him more than it hurt him believe it or not. He's got a unique look. It is not just his natural features it is also his style of dress that is distinctive.

Cartoonists really enjoyed lampooning him and for this reason and others, it kept Mr Trump in the news and in the minds of voters. They loved his hair most of all but other features such as his hands, mouth, teeth and cheeks are also distinctive. Mr Trump's body size also helped. He was the anti-Obama in more ways than one. For example, where Obama was thin and gaunt, Mr Trump was big and robust. Mr Trump had an all American body type that implied he enjoys a good steak and hamburger from time to time – and he didn't work out. It showed in his face and stomach. And for many Americans who struggle with weight issues, it made him more relatable.

Thus even when cartoonists attempt to exaggerate his appearance it only enhanced their love for Trump who many have come to view as a hero.

## 12. **Befriend Your Potential Enemies**

Mr Trump was probably petrified of Russian president Vladimir Putin and saw in Putin, a kindred spirit if not a dangerous match. What did Trump do? He turned the fear into admiration and praise. He took advantage of the media exposure he was receiving to send messages to the Russian president repeatedly saying "I will get along with him; he will respect me; he doesn't respect Obama but he and I will get along great."

Mr Trump was extremely careful never to criticize Mr Putin publicly. He had no qualms about criticizing others such as the Chinese and the Mexicans. But he remained deferential to the Russian president and many people viewed this as him very skilfully turning a potential enemy into a friend.

Other Republican challengers like Carly Fiorina and Marco Rubio went in the opposite direction by harshly criticizing the Russian leader but not Trump. And word on the street was that Putin was also having his own lovefest with Mr Trump. Mr Trump befriended his domestic enemies as well. Who can forget that high five that Mr Trump gave to Jeb Bush in the CNN debate? It was incredibly effective. After that, hardly ever did you hear Jeb Bush criticize Mr Trump in the media.

## 13.Have a Hot Spouse and an Even Hotter Daughter

Obviously, it is you who is running for president and not your spouse but it doesn't hurt to have a Trump card. In 2005, Mr Trump married his third wife Melania Knauss. Ms Knauss was a gorgeous model from Slovenia who was more than twenty-five years his junior, and who had impeccable manners to match her looks. Some people called her a trophy wife others called her a gold digger. Whatever you call her is up to you but there is no question that she was Mr Trump's trump card.

Before Melania, Trump had had two other reasonably gorgeous wives: a Czech ski champion (wife number one) and a Georgia peach (wife number two). Either of these women would have also probably helped his image but not as effectively as

Melania. At the same time, Melania was bested by another woman in Trump's life. Of his oldest daughter Ivanka Trump he has said "Ivanka is very beautiful…" He certainly has impeccable taste in women and knew how to parade them at the most well-timed intervals.

This created intrigue and ignited the curiosity and adoration of the voyeurs. Other men salivated when they beheld the Trump women and they couldn't but respect Mr Trump even more. This translated into higher poll numbers.

## 14. **Use Third Grade Level Vocabulary**

Mr Trump understood instinctively that most people prefer simple language and appreciate simple words. Though he has a college level education, he never tried to laud a superior vocabulary over people. When he talked, even a third grader could understand. This quality had broad appeal with diverse demographic groups – even the highly educated set who appreciated the simplicity of Trump's message and preferred to eschew more pedantic candidates whose message arguably required too much analysis and deliberation.

This is not to say that Mr Trump was not a very smart guy with a very high level vocabulary. He must be because he went to the Wharton School of Economics and he is used to hanging around a lot of very bright people. But he did not seem to feel the need to flaunt his superior intellect and vocabulary. He preferred instead to speak in a way that both blue collar and white collar people of any social strata could understand.

### 15. Wing it (Just See What Develops)

Mr Trump famously said that he was not a "debater" and that he would not prepare for the debates like the other candidates did. He dismissed the other candidates as good debaters who were all talk and no action. Instead, he lowered expectations for his debate performance saying that he had never debated before but that he was a doer and a job creator, not a debater.

It was apparent that he had not prepared for the worst case scenario because minutes into the first presidential debate of the 2016 race he was asked the famous question by journalist Megyn Kelly: "You have called women you don't like fat pigs, disgusting animals, dogs..." To which Mr Trump deadpanned: "Only Rosie O'Donnell. Excuse me." This could have cost him the debate but many viewers said he won the debate for the very fact that he was not scripted and he responded spontaneously to that and other questions.

## 16. Never Use Teleprompters

Mr Trump has often ridiculed politicians who use tele-prompters and he has boasted that he never used tele-prompters. And he did have a point. Politicians who use tele-prompters are obviously not being spontaneous. They are relying on written speeches which are often written by others.

Mr Trump liked to shoot from the hips even though most of his speeches ended up sounding the same so it was clear that he had an original script which he memorized and so there usually was no need for tele prompters. Additionally, he always seemed to carry a cheat sheet in his pocket which he invariably took out before beginning his speech. How did this help him win points with voters? Well, if his high poll numbers meant anything, then clearly voters did not want a scripted candidate. They liked the element of surprise and spontaneity. It was like listening to a stand-up comedian. You didn't know what was coming but you fully expected it was going to be good. Of course, later on, he pulled out the tele-prompter.

## 17. Fire Your Entire Campaign Staff Before the First Primary and Caucus if they get on your nerves

Very early in his campaign Mr Trump fired his top, trusted adviser Roger Stone. Mr Stone immediately denied he had been fired and instead says that he quit the campaign because he felt the campaign and become a "food fight" and that Mr Trump was "off message." Whatever the truth is, a key adviser left the campaign in the early months, along with a couple of other staffers and right after Mr Trump's message seemed to become clearer and began to resonate even louder. He even began to discuss policy ideas and issues like Tax, Immigration and Foreign Policy.

Many people credit the shake up that took place behind the scenes for jolting Mr Trump back on message, demonstrating that in the end, almost anyone can be rendered redundant and irrelevant. And poor Mr Stone spent the ensuing months giving Mr Trump free publicity by praising him every chance he got on various chat shows. This, of course, was only the beginning.

## 18. Hire Scary Lawyers and PR People To Defend You, If needed

Mr Trump had some henchmen and lieutenants who seemed willing to do and say anything to protect him and to intimidate and censor anyone who would dare criticize him or disclose any secrets of his personal or public life. This is an important aspect of running for public office because people will say and do anything to derail your campaign and it is critical that they fear you so they stop before they even begin.

Whether it was threats of the financial of physical nature, would-be offenders would be set straight if not by Mr Trump himself then by one of his hired guns. This included aggressive lawyers who would threaten to sue for a crippling sum and security guards who would literally take signs away from protesters outside of Trump Tower. The fact that Trump had his private army was enough to silence would be attackers since few people had the financial wherewithal to take on Mr Trump and his legal team and band of security personnel.

### 19.Gain a psychological edge early

Mr Trump muscled his way to the top of the opinion polls fairly early in the campaign and maintained this advantage for a significant period of time before he began to fall. This enabled him to gain a psychological advantage very early on and being the one to beat, he commanded

deference and respect from other candidates

and from the media.

His rivals were inviting themselves out

to lunch with him and to play golf; they were

asking him to mention them in media

interviews; they were threading carefully

with him, realizing that once the campaign

was over, if he won, there could be certain

benefits if he viewed them as a friend rather

than foe. But staying at the top of the polls

also gained him the respect and admiration

of the media, many of whom ridiculed him in the beginning. Now they were tripping over themselves trying to get exclusive interviews and in person chats with the candidate. This solidified his status as frontrunner for some time as voters continued to view him favourably when compared to his rivals.

### 20. Use Your Private Residence (which must be posh) as Your Campaign Headquarters

Trump Tower as campaign headquarters gave Trump a movie star edge over the other candidates that was hard for them to compete with. This tony Manhattan address was a comprehensive package that included a shiny campaign store where people (including international tourists) could learn more about the candidate and buy his memorabilia and books. Knowing that the candidate lived just upstairs in his own gilded version of the palace of Versailles also added to the allure and fantasy, further propelling his mythic candidacy upwards.

The irony is that the actual campaign headquarters were on a floor of Trump Tower that could not get any more raw and "unposh." An exposé was done of his campaign headquarters to show that it was a glorified warehouse and people who were working on his campaign showed up to work hard, not lap luxury on his 757. But there was definitely this image of glamour that most people conjured when they imagined his headquarters at Trump Tower. Indeed, his was the only campaign headquarters that the average American knew exactly where it was located. This only made Trump more iconic

21. **Threaten to Run Independent if the Party You Are Running Under Fails To Treat You "Fairly"**

There is no better way to keep your party bosses in line than to threaten to run an independent campaign if you don't get your way. Trump's naked threat of running as an independent if not treated "fairly" by the Republican Party helped him control Republican party bosses and gave him room to develop his campaign and grow his base.

Whereas party heads could have excoriated him in the press and spread rumors and tales designed to sour voter confidence and regard, because they were deathly afraid of the consequences of an independent run by Mr Trump, they behaved themselves and, at least publicly, treated him fairly and with respect and deference. In the end, of course, he signed the pledge not to run as an independent. But everyone knew that the pledge was not a contract and so party bosses stayed on their toes, careful not to rock the boat, lest Mr Trump should run independent and thus guarantee victory for the Democrats.

### 22. Give Out Your Opponent's Private Cell Phone Number on National TV (and pull other pranks)

Early in the campaign, Trump gave out the private cell phone number of one of his opponents on national television. I think it was Lindsey Graham. Not only was this unexpected and therefore took everyone by surprise (and maybe even shocked a few people), it also added to Trump's bad boy take no prisoner persona and showed that he also had a playful side that was willing to flout convention.

In response, an American website, Gawker, published Trump's private cell phone number but Trump just casually turned that around by putting an automatic campaign message on the phone so that callers could hear more about the Trump campaign and learn more about what the candidate wanted to do as President. Win win for Trump.

### 23. Sleep As Little As Possible

Mr Trump has said in at least one of his books that he requires very little sleep and it must have been true because during the campaign it became clear very quickly that he was up in the wee hours of the morning sending tweets (sometimes angry ones) on Twitter. Yet, even when staying up till way past three in the morning, by seven he often was up and calling in to radio shows. This twenty four hour cycle he kept enabled him to keep up on all the news while others were sleeping. He knew what was going on in the rest of the world and what was being said about him in various media including blogs, TV shows and online newspapers.

This enabled him to personally respond in real time to perceived or real threats to his campaign and to nip problems in the bud long before other candidates prone to sleep would have been able to. It is a good idea for any future presidential candidate to follow this rule. The key is to look refreshed in the aftermath. It is okay to sleep as little as possible but you can't look like you are not getting enough sleep. Nobody is going to vote for a tired looking president. It does beg the question: How did Trump do it?

### 24. Master the Art of The Pivot

Pivoting may not have been his strongest skill initially but as time went by,

Mr Trump got better and better at it. So that when he was attacked on an issue, or when a scathing and potentially damaging report was written about him, or when another challenger accused him of something that could damage his credibility as a candidate, he became better and better at getting out of the cul de sac often times by throwing someone else under the bus.

So for example when Rand Paul ran ads questioning his conservatism, Trump mocked Paul as an inferior golf player who had no prayer of winning the election. During the Cleveland debate, he humiliated Rand Paul by questioning why he was even in the race given his low poll numbers. When it looked like his goose was cooked with the Megyn Kelly comment he assured everyone that he cherished women and pointed out that Jeb Bush was the real problem for saying he (Jeb) would not spend too much on women's health issues he then assured the nation that his wife Melania would join him on the campaign trail to assist him with discussing

women's issues.  True, she never did. But so
what?

### 25.Donate to Politicians From Both Parties Then Publicly Shame The Recipients of Your Cash

One of the themes of the 2016
election was the fact that Washington
politicians were in bed with rich business
people who donated enormous sums to
presidential and other political campaigns

in exchange for various favours. Trump apparently received lots of favours from various politicians to whom he had given a lot of money over the years.

During the campaign he had no qualms about outing all the politicians he had given money to over the years. Plenty of the 2016 candidates were shamed speechless as a result. This included candidates from both political parties.

The public shaming of candidates like Democrat Hillary Clinton who Trump said he "ordered" to attend his wedding (a favour in exchange for his campaign contribution apparently) had a chilling effect on their ability to really go after the real estate tycoon with any real zeal. It rendered them spectators in the Trump Show. Everyone was cautious about how they thread with Mr Trump. It was as if he knew their deepest darkest secrets and they were petrified of rubbing him the wrong way lest he should spill the beans to the entire world. So this is a good offensive strategy.

## 26.Make Big Promises Even If You Can't Keep Them

During the campaign, Mr Trump's promises were big, bold and bombastic. The biggest was that he would build a wall between the United States and Mexico to keep out illegal aliens many of whom, in his words, were "rapists" and "criminals." But even more outrageously, he said he would make Mexico pay for that wall. I am convinced that he knew at the time he made these promises that most of these promises could not be kept. But that is not the point. The point with winning elections seem to be that you tell the people what they want to hear. You promise them what you think they want and if you are elected, you just break the promise and say you're sorry.

There were other promises including that he would bring back jobs from China and Mexico and go into Iraq and "bomb the shit out of ISIS" take their oil and give contracts to Exxon Mobile and other Giant energy companies to rebuild and re-establish order. How would he achieve this? He would just "bomb the hell out of them." People loved this kind of rhetoric and this and other things drove Mr Trump's poll numbers up like a rocket, notwithstanding the fact that most experts and pundits opined at the time that these initiatives had almost zero possibility of actually happening. They obviously missed the point.

What was most important was energizing his base with the thought that these things could actually happen, and that, Mr Trump did better than anyone else running against him.

## 27.Have Head of Full of Iconic Hair

Mr Trump certainly did not create his hair for the campaign (he's had his crop for decades) and he has been heavily mocked for his hair for decades. So much so that his hair became a part of his image, a part of his brand. During the campaign his hair took on a higher level of global celebrity but ironically, he seemed to really have managed it exceptionally well and even though he had one of his fans prove the authenticity of his locks at a rally, his hair was not ridiculed half as much as it usually was. Hardly ever was he caught having a bad hair day or a bad hair moment during the campaign. The comb over was there as usual, but it was very well tailored and very well tamed. During the campaign his hair also gained international traction as more people around the world became aware of Mr Trump.

Some foreigners on social media made comments like "I thought that was photo shopped!" The thing with the improbable hair is it just added to his larger than life persona and it was something else that helped him to stand out. It made him noticeable and the center of conversation. For people competing and trying to outshine their competition, it is important to have something like your hair that is uniquely you. No, you don't need to have a comb over but you do need to do something interesting and distinctive with your hair.

### 28. Have a Catchy Campaign Slogan

What were the campaign slogans for the presidential hopefuls in the 2016 campaign? Did Jeb Bush have a campaign slogan? What about Marco Rubio and Rand Paul? How about Bernie Sanders? Hillary did later on "Stronger Together!" But what about the others? Did they have campaign slogans? If they did they certainly didn't plug it as much as Trump did. From day one Mr Trump's slogan was "Make America Great Again."

He probably took a page from Obama's playbook. Decades later if you ask what Obama's campaign was all about, the buzz word is "Change." Trump understood the power of having the right buzzwords. In no time, due to his constant repetition of it, most Americans could and were reciting Mr Trump's slogan. This brilliant marketing strategy alone helped to lend gravitas and credibility to Trump very early in the campaign. He repeated it every chance he got and then other candidates and potential voters, children, as well as the media began to repeat it. It was smart of him to trademark his slogan because it had such mass market appeal that other candidates would surely have stolen it if only they could.

## 29. Admit To An Erratic Voting Record By Comparing it To A Past President

"I have evolved" Mr Trump would retort every time one of his opponents tried to use his erratic voting history against him. The guy had been a registered Democrat,

Republican and Independent more times than any one in recent memory. But he explained it away as something that even great presidents like Ronald Reagan had done and this shut everyone up. It is not just the voting record that he admitted to.

Mr Trump would take any situation that could completely derail another candidate and turn it into a win. He even said that he was a guy who was used to winning and that when he didn't win he found a way to turn the loss into a win. The takeaway for the rest of us is the same: if your opponent

finds your weak spot and tries to use it

against you, just admit the weakness but then

pivot and turn it into a strength by attaching

it to someone who is well-respected in your

domain.

### 30. Strategically Lower Expectations While Simultaneously Raising Expectations

Mr Trump can be accused of many

things but being an idiot is not one of them.

Sure he made outlandish promises but he

would very subtle insert from time to time "this is going to be hard because we are in such deep trouble." The key is to know when and where to say it. People shouldn't readily be able to discern it; it has to be in the subtext.

Mr Trump is very skilled with peppering his speech with subtext that most people miss in the verbal seduction of his naked words. He made big outlandish promises (raised expectations) but then he threw in a disclaimer that the listener would probably miss; but if needed, in the future, he could always say "I never said that." Another way he did that was to divulge that he had an exit strategy just in case things did not work out, while remaining careful to say that he would win the race.

## 31. Do Not Fundraise

When Trump burst onto the presidential scene, he boldly asserted "I am rich. I don't need anybody's money." In fact, he made much of the fact that his challengers were all taking money from special interest donors and that they would become beholden to these donors to the detriment of the interest of average Americans.

As time went on, however, Mr Trump because to solicit donations explaining that he would match each dollar donated with his own money. He further explained that the donations are for the psychological edge to show that people really cared about him as a candidate; that it was not a question of need. Later on in the contest he rejected super PACs and denounced their money. He clearly was not comfortable with overtly soliciting and accepting cash through fundraising sources. But make no mistake about it. Trump supporters still sent money to the campaign and they purchased campaign items like the iconic "make America great again" baseball cap. So there are ways to fundraise without looking like you are fundraising. Trump was a master at this.

## 32. Make It Up As You Go Along (Just See What Develops)

Trump was heavily criticized in the beginning for seemingly not having his policies fleshed out on such issues as foreign policy, immigration and Trade. He kept telling the media that he would get back to them at a later time with fleshed out policy objectives.

As time went on he hired and teamed with the most highly respected people in the various disciplines, including U.S. Senator Sessions who helped him with his immigration plan and undisclosed experts who helped him flesh out his tax plan which was widely praised in many circles (though criticized in others.)

The key point is that he did not have fleshed out plans on day one but developed them after a few months on the trail. This gave him an opportunity to learn the lay of the land and to listen to a lot of different ideas from different people. By the time he disclosed some of his proposals, like his tax plan, for example, it helped to push him further up in the polls (just as he was starting to fall).

But as of the writing of this book, the elections are still one year away. So there is no way of knowing how well this strategy will turn out in the end. Mr Trump for example has been heavily criticised for not having laid out campaign infrastructure that will enable him to win a national election. Many experts predict he will lose the election for this very habit he tends to have of "making it up as he goes along.

## 33. Hire a Young, Hungry, Inexperienced Campaign Manager

Trump's Campaign manager was a young inexperienced New Englander named Corey Lewandowki who was described in some circles as a "bomb thrower." Corey was a loyal soldier to Mr Trump (at least up until this writing he has been). He often appeared on television to defend one or the other policy idea of his client/boss.

For several months he was the only campaign manager who was getting any press. No one knew who was running the campaigns of other candidates but they knew Corey by name. This was because he was hungry and wanted to succeed both for himself and for his client. He knew instinctively that if Trump won he would become a heavyweight in the political arena and he worked really hard for Trump as a result. (Of course, Trump ended up firing him).

## 34. Be Frugal

Mr Trump started his campaign by telling everyone that he was rich. He even had a piece of paper to show it and he dangled this in the air for maximum effect during his campaign début. Yet when it came time to spend money, he did not do a headlong plunge. In fact, one is his advisors complained publicly that Trump would not give him money to do a "scientific poll."

Also, Trump was slow to buy TV ads instead content to do as many television and print interviews as possible (he even sat down with People Magazine) and called into as many radio shows, as well as exploited social media to keep himself in front of viewers. He did go to other events such as the Iowa state fair to shake hands and eat corn dogs. As time went on, he began to sell campaign hats and tee shirts and baby apparel to raise money and later still, he did an about face and began to solicit donations from donors.

And yes, eventually he turned to TV ads. But through it all, he remained frugal.

He did not spend like a fool. He watched his pennies though he is rumoured to have paid his campaign staff at better rates than his competitors. He splurged there. But otherwise it was penny-pinching all the way. No wonder the guy had a networth of nearly ten billion dollars!

### 35. Intimidate Your Critics By Suing People left and right

Nobody used the legal system better than Trump both before and during his run for president. This guy has always known how to use the laws to his maximum benefit whether it was the bankruptcy laws or the civil laws.

On the former he was perfectly open about filing for corporate bankruptcy 4 times to take advantage of the chapter laws to benefit himself and his companies. He has never really articulated his motivation for his civil law suits but often he sues for millions of dollars (and wins) for defamation or breach of contract. People have openly described him as a litigious guy.

During the campaign he had at least 4 lawsuits in progress against persons or companies that had either breached contracts or made utterances against him that he perceived to be untrue (and his family members had a few as well). He even had one going on in Scotland! Knowing this, would be defamers or critics threaded very carefully. They checked and fact checked their statements before publishing them. Often, even when they had the facts and it was potentially damaging to Mr Trump they either published it reluctantly – never really driving the point home too hard – or declined to publish it at all. So his opponents gained no advantages even from his dirt. This was the power of Trump.

## 36. Pay Actors, if necessary

Mr Trump is alleged to have paid actors to populate the crowd when he announced his intention to run for the presidency of the United States from his Trump Tower address in Manhattan in June 2015. But this was not necessary for very long. In fact, he probably only had to do that once. Afterwards, it was standing room only at his events and often times there was overflow and people had to be kept outside.

The lesson is, initially, it may be necessary to fake it till it's true. Faking it could mean faking supporters, faking crowds, faking an audience. This breeds success because the more people and supporters you seem to have, the more people and supporters you will be able to attract to your events. Because, really, during elections, people sometimes act like sheep. They do and go and support who their friends, neighbors and contemporaries support. So you need to get them in order to hook them and for that it may be necessary to pay them, at least initially.

## 37.Be upfront about not liking to shake hands

It is no secret that Mr Trump hates to shake hands. He has said so himself in his own books and during interviews. It is also no secret that in politics and particularly when campaigning, shaking hands is a must. The trick here is to build a reputation before-hand so that people know that you are germ-o-phobic who does not like to shake hands. This way they won't take it personally that you scorned them and thus, decline to vote for you; they will know it is just how you are with everyone – it is not personal. If you are planning a presidential run, you really have to think about this and you really have to make it known beforehand that you are not into shaking hands.

If you don't make this known in advance and you refuse to shake hands, you will look cold and unfriendly and will lose the trust and acceptance of the voting populace. Truth be told, if you are entering public life you probably should get over this fear and just go ahead and shake the hands.

But if you really just can't stand it, you have to make light of it beforehand.

### 38.Blame Other Countries for Your Own Countries Economic Troubles

Americans are some of the most patriotic people in the world. They love their country and they love the idea of being number one in every way but in particular economically. There probably is no other nation of people who have ever enjoyed their number one status in the world than Americans.

But lately America has had its share of economic problems. What Mr Trump was able to do was to give Americans someone to blame for things like manufacturing jobs which, as he correctly identified, were going to China and South America. He argued that this put some Americans out of work and ultimately contributed to weakening rather than strengthening the economy.

Mr Trump identified the countries by name and promised Americans he would bring the jobs home from places like China and Mexico. These new jobs he promised would go to Hispanics and others he had insulted over the years. He won huge points with this finger-pointing technique and then with the promise that he would be able to make them better off economically by standing up to these countries.

### 39. Promise to be a bomb thrower

Mr Trump had a major beef with ISIS and he promised to invade Iraq if elected, "bomb the hell out of them," and take their oil. His supporters loved this message. He also promised to hand it to countries like China, Mexico and Iran. He got huge kudos from his base for these promises. The idea of this type of aggressive action was like an invitation to witness a boxing match and it excited people. His rallies attracted huge crowds and he got many standing ovations.

People appreciated Mr Trump's tough talk and as a general rule, unless you are looking for a yoga teacher as well as a meditation guru, understand that folks tend to prefer tough-talking leaders to pacifists. This might explain the appeal a guy like Vladimir Putin had in Russia. Even Mr Trump deferred to him – a fact worth noting because he was just about the only person that Mr Trump deferred to. The bold statements he made were definitely good for Mr Trump's poll numbers. People really respected him, it seems.

## 40. Promise to Create Jobs (For Ethnic Groups After You Insult them)

One of the most surprising things in the 2016 elections was the high percentages of Blacks and Hispanics that polled positively for Trump. This was counterintuitive for a lot of people but it made perfect sense. Even though he had said many controversial things about Mexicans, Mr Trump was smart enough to understand that you do catch bees with honey and when it comes to jobs for low income groups and immigrants, obviously the best honey is actually having work to provide for their families.

Mr Trump exploited this very well. At every turn he promised to create a ton of jobs and to bring jobs back from Mexico and China. He told them what they wanted to hear. By October 2015 he was getting more than 25 percent of the black vote in polls and again, he targeted black business and chambers of commerce catering to black populations.

It was not a hard sell because the guy had made himself several billions as a private sector entrepreneur and both African American and Hispanic communities who traditionally have been on the lower end of the economic spectrum in mainstream American communities really seemed to like what he was saying about jobs.

How this will all play out is not clear as of the writing of this book however the lesson is to make big promises to disadvantaged groups, get them converted, and worry about delivering it later.

## 41.Constantly Tell the Media They Suck

Mr Trump was not shy about excoriating the media at every turn. This only served to incite the media, create a frenzy, keep them on their toes and make Mr Trump more media catnip. Why? Because the media is not used to being publicly shamed and they really respected

Mr Trump's audacity, they really feared him. They almost seemed to love him more when he spanked them, actually.

They say some people like to be abused (for example masochists) and when it came to Mr Trump, the media really seemed to be at the receiving end of his whip of a tongue. Mr Trump was also very skilled about playing a hot and cold game with certain media outlets, sometimes ignoring the journalists from that outlet, blacklisting them and giving exclusives to other competitors, or boycotting the entire network.

This kept the media at his beck and call and competing to get those exclusives with him because they all wanted his interviews. Of course in order to get the exclusives it meant that the media outlet had to "behave nicely" towards Mr Trump.

The advantage was obvious. This control over the media and what was said about him and how he was treated enabled Mr Trump to perpetuate this image of power and toughness. Before you know it, as early as October 2015 even former president Bill Clinton was saying in interviews that he thought Mr Trump had done a great job of branding himself and that he thought Mr Trump could actually win the election (even though he was careful to say that he and Mr Trump were "former friends" and this did not surprise anyone given how Mr

Trump went after Hillary Clinton who was the frontrunner on the Democratic side and obviously wife of Mr Clinton.)

### 42. **Whine a Lot**

Mr Trump is a self-confessed, unapologetic whiner. He has said "I am a whiner and I will whine until I win." The minute he felt he was being treated "unfairly" especially in the media, he complained about it. He complained a lot, constantly calling out members of the press for slights, misquotes and unfair treatment. This tendency won him the dubious reputation of being a whiner but it was very effective because once the media saw that he wasn't going to take the treatment lying down, they really seemed to pull up their socks and were very careful and deferential to Mr Trump.

They routinely referred to him as "Mr Trump" and some even called him "President Trump" which was interesting considering that even after Obama won the presidential election, no one in the media ever once made that mistake of calling him President Obama till the day he was sworn in and took office. Instead they called him the "President Elect." This is how powerful whining can be for some folks. Truth be told, this strategy may not have worked for a guy like Obama and it won't work for everyone but if you are someone who can get away with it, then by all means use this strategy to its full advantage.

### 43.Hire A Sexy Assistant

Throughout his campaign (and really before he even launched his campaign) Mr Trump is rumoured to have hired a gorgeous young assistant to fly around the world with him and take his dictation. Her name was Hope Hicks at the time she was about 26 years old.

During the campaign she was sometimes photographed slipping out of his helicopter in stockings and high heels, or in the side pews with her cell phone and a notepad handy, ready at Mr Trump's beck and call. She was rarely if ever photographed with a strand of hair out of place. She was quoted a lot on various issues by various sources but she still managed to keep a very low profile outside of her job. One media personality described her as someone who always "kept her head down."

It is very possible that young Ms Hicks was one of Mr Trump's secret weapons (or Trump cards) who helped to keep him organized and who was his eyes and ears and other things. In other words she was an asset who along with other strong women surrounding the candidate like his wife and daughters helped to propel his campaign to the top of the polls from very early in the process.

## 44. Load Up on Energy

Whatever he was eating, drinking, smoking or inhaling during the campaign we will never know but the one thing for certain is that Mr Trump had the most energy of the entire campaign, among all the candidates, even though he was one of the oldest participants, was not in particularly great physical shape, and even though he seemed to get the least amount of sleep - given his propensity for sending late night tweets.

Indeed, the only time he ever seemed tired was during the three hour debate in Cleveland. It was the first time

Mr Trump had looked tired in public. He even broke out in a sweat and afterwards he was mocked by many pundits who said he looked his age for the first time.

This obviously incensed Mr Trump who rebuked CNN for carrying on the debate longer than the movie *Gone With The Wind*. Still, it was one of the few times that Mr Trump was less than energetic and he really emphasized the importance of having energy during the campaign.

Truth be told, one of the reasons he probably seemed so energetic was because he so often mocked Jeb Bush who admittedly was a slower-paced person by nature. What can a person do if they are slower by nature? Well, I guess for Trump there is no excuse for being slow-paced. So just don't be low energy. Inhale something.

### 45. Be a Bully

If you ask Mr Trump, chances are he would never admit to being a bully but the description has been used to describe him by a diverse number of individuals from both political parties. If he heard them we will never know because even if he never admitted to being a bully, he also has never openly denied being a bully nor has he objected to the moniker.

While Mr Trump usually went after people who attacked him verbally, there were many instances where he seems to have been on the offensive. That is, he attacked without provocation from the victim, for example in the cases of Mitt Romney and Barack Obama. Mr Trump expressed no shame about this and in fact, it is quite possible that he deliberately took this aggressive posture to instill fear and to send a message to others that if they messed with him or if they ran afoul of his good graces they too would be mercilessly bullied, taunted and drawn into a mud fight.

Most people seemed to prefer not having to be on the receiving end of Mr Trump's ire and disdain. Therefore, they just automatically behaved. It was amazing.

### 46. Master the Art of Multiple Personalities

Mr Trump received a lot of criticism that he was "unpredictable" and that he had supported different political parties at different times in his life. Indeed on of his republican challengers Rand Paul released some TV ads showing Mr Trump praising

the Democratic Party and admitting that he
felt the economy does better under the
Democrats.

He was also shown on video praising
Democratic challenger Hillary Clinton as a
capable politician and secretary of state even
though during the campaign he has said that
she had been "the worse secretary of state the
country has ever seen" and he also said that
her email controversy was a "criminal
matter" that would knock her out of the race.
How did he handle the potentially damaging

pieces of work? He simply said "I have evolved."

But there were times when Mr Trump didn't even try to explain his inconsistencies. One minute he is saying that CNN did a great job with the debate the next he was saying they did a terrible job. One minute his is pro-life the next he is pro-choice. One minute he loves the Chinese people and the next he would feed the Chinese president hamburgers rather than give him a state dinner. He was all over the map. It kept the attention focused squarely on him and not on any of his competitors. And like he always boasts: "any press is good press.

## 47.Be Unpredictable

Mr Trump was totally unpredictable during the campaign. Some might have said he was predictably unpredictable and this also was true. You never knew which way the wind would blow with him; you never knew what he would say or do next; you never knew who he would attack. What you did know for sure and what you could predict was that with Mr Trump something was always up.

There was never a dull moment. For example, just when you thought his feud with Megyn Kelly was done, he would reignite it again. Just when you thought he and Jeb Bush had kissed and made up, he attacked Jeb's brother saying "911 happened on George Bush's watch." Just when you thought he hated Hillary, he praised her performance in the first debate. Just when you thought he was the most military guy out there who loved and admired Vladimir Putin, he said America should stay out of Syria and let Putin handle it alone. Just when you thought he would insult Carly Fiorina he said she was beautiful. And the list goes on.

The point is you couldn't ever tell whether he was coming or going or whether he would be hot or cold. The result was that he commanded a lot of attention and this kept his poll numbers very high without him having to spend any money.

### 48. Promise to lower taxes for everyone

Nobody likes to pay taxes and nobody understood this like Trump. Even he hates to pay taxes. He has bragged on more than one occasion that he "fights like hell to pay as little taxes as possible." So when he unveiled his tax plan in the fall of 2015 that promised to lower the tax rate for all individuals and corporations, it was catnip for the entire country. Everybody loved the idea.

Trump was careful not to say like George H.W. Bush: "read my lips; no new taxes." He probably was planning a whole bunch of new taxes to make up for any deficits created by his tax plan even while he was unveiling his plan. But this was a secondary issue. The first level was telling the American people that they would pay *less* taxes (and in some cases *none* at all) under his plan. The idea was uniformly embraced even if it amounted to nothing but a fantasy. It sent his contenders scrambling but none of them ever came out and panned the plan. Nor did they offer one that was better; and whereas Trump was starting to slide down in the polls right before this, after he disclosed this catnip he started to climb back up the polls again.

## 49. Don't Hesitate to Dig Up and Release
### All the Dirt You Can Find On Your Enemies

More than once, as a defensive move, Mr Trump had to pull out dirt on his detractors and critics and disclose then on his twitter account so that his supporters and enemies alike could get a load of the dirt, thereby censoring his enemy. One example was when the controversy involving Fox News Megyn Fox was at its height. Trump had just made the blood comment and his adviser Roger Stone had just quit. Things were falling apart quick and he had to do major damage control.

What did he do? He pulled up the dirt on an interview Kelly had done with Howard

Stone writing "See, I am the pure one" and published it on Twitter. Within hours of this, Fox News reportedly went crawling to Mr Trump to promise him he would be treated "fairly." Another time he pulled out the dirt, again with the Megyn/Fox controversy when he was disinvited to a Red State Conference in Georgia with organizer Erick Erickson. Erickson said he was sickened by Trump's comments and did not want Trump at his event or in a room with his wife and daughter.

What did Trump do? He dug up tweets and other dirt on Erickson showing Erickson to be a major chauvinist who had used less than respectful language against women. This too was splattered all over Mr Trump's social media accounts. The result? Erickson grew silent and within days Megyn Kelly announced she was taking a 10 day vacation and Trump flew off to the Iowa fair to give little kids who called him "batman" a tour of and on his eponymous helicopter. Of course that works both ways. Dirt also flew about

Mr. Trump and his wives – especially Melania, his third wife. But he just completely ignored all that.

## 50. Have an Exit Strategy Long Before you Need it

Trump began to drop hints about a possible exit from the race in October 2015. He was doing an interview on a Sunday morning talk show and he basically said, "I am not a masochist. If I start to tank I will quit and go back to my business. Why would I continue if I am not doing well?" The press had a field day and began to speculate that an exit was imminent.

Trump was quick to clear things up. No, it is not he was actively considering quitting but he was simply letting it be known that he did not need the job and did not want the job so bad that his life would fall apart if he didn't get it. He had options and he wanted everyone to know that if things imploded, it wasn't going to be a big problem for him. This was a very smart move on his part and one that you should definitely mimic if you are ever in the same position. And guess what? It doesn't even have to be running for president. You can use these techniques in other contexts as well.

The key is to let them know you don't care if you lose.

**Cover Photo from Flickr**

https://www.flickr.com/photos/gageskidmore/25146024234/in/photolist-Ej4WVY-9kwYUn-sMpybD-DfxDqn-DDs81c-DKPp3W-EcWu8a-E2uYpE-EcWudv-DfdaL3-E4GbnT-HndmbC-JbJqWV-HnioAg-Jiju7c-HnkKsT-J9rG3o-J9q3dY-HndrBC-HSKeeG-HnjQVD-J9rbc1-Je89Lm-HneXD9-C6udkQ-BNWjHC-BiHMv8-C6ww1q-BGBPZr-BNYyv3-BNWFAu-BNWJKL-BiHTPk-9hHpJr-HUtSBa-Cg5eLB-BNZ3hL-BiyDcy-BiFBtt-C6tV3J-BGy26H-BiC1bG-C6xb7A-Cg4Csv-Cg4EBv-

CdNqkh-C8Pssr-C6uA6y-CdP4D5-BiHk5c

www.ingramcontent.com/pod-product-compliance
Lightning Source LLC
Chambersburg PA
CBHW080947050426
42337CB00055B/4576